The Lessons of
Azusa
Street
on
Revival

LARRY KEEFAUVER,
GENERAL EDITOR

CREATION
HOUSE
Orlando, FL

THE LESSONS OF AZUSA STREET ON REVIVAL
A Charisma Classics Bible Study
Larry Keefauver, General Editor
Published by Creation House
Strang Communications Company
600 Rinehart Road
Lake Mary, Florida 32746
Web site: http://www.creationhouse.com

Unless otherwise noted, all Scripture quotations are from the
King James Version of the Bible.

Scripture quotations marked NLT are from the Holy Bible,
New Living Translation, copyright © 1996.
Used by permission of Tyndale House Publishers, Inc.,
Wheaton, IL 60189. All rights reserved.

Contents

Introduction

WELCOME TO THIS devotional study guide on *The Lessons of Azusa Street on Revival*. This study is a companion volume to *The Original Azusa Street Devotional*.

This devotional study is part of a series of four Bible study guides focused on the teachings of some of the founding leaders of the Spirit-filled and Pentecostal movements—Smith Wigglesworth, John G. Lake, Maria Woodworth-Etter, and William J. Seymour from Azusa Street. Do not feel that you must go through this series in any particular order. Choose the guides and sequence that best meets your spiritual needs.

We wish to share briefly some information about the Azusa Street revival and its primary figure—Willam J. Seymour. William J. Seymour had been an evangelist in Mississippi, then pastored a Holiness congregation in Houston prior to his arrival in Los Angeles in early 1906 to pastor an African-American congregation led by Julia W. Hutchins.

While in Mississippi, he was influenced by people who had been under the ministry of Charles Parham, a white minister in Topeka, Kansas, who was called the founder of Pentecostalism. Parham had founded a Bible School where he and his students, starting with Agnes M. Ozman, were baptized with the Spirit and spoke in tongues.

Believing in the baptism of the Spirit with the evidence of speaking in tongues, Seymour provoked the ire of some of the congregation with his Pentecostal teaching. Not only did this bold, black evangelist preach holiness and divine healing at his church in Los Angeles, he also began preaching about the Holy Spirit's baptism. Locked out of the church one April evening, he was welcomed into the home of Mr. and Mrs. Edward Lee where he began conducting house meetings. On April 9, 1906, Seymour prayed for Lee's healing. Not only was Edward Lee healed, he also began speaking in tongues and started to testify to others about his experience. Later that same day, seven more people were baptized in the Spirit and spoke in tongues. On April 12, 1906, Seymour himself experienced the same baptism.

The interracial house meetings grew to such a size that they were moved to a two-story frame livery stable that had in its early days been a church building. By late April, the building, which could seat about 750 persons, was ready for meetings. Within days, revival broke out attracting people from all over the world. On April 18, 1906, the *Los Angeles Daily Times* reported the revival with a front-page story. During approximately one thousand days of revival, tens of thousands from around the world came to Azusa Street and were touched by the fiery outpouring of the Holy Spirit. This revival is considered by many to be the torch that ignited worldwide, Pentecostal revival in the twentieth century.

Pentecostal theology had its roots in nineteenth century fundamentalism with such key leaders as Charles Finney, R. A. Torrey, A. J. Gordon, and many others who spoke of the enduement of power by the Spirit, divine healing, and the imminent return of Christ. These Holiness streams led to a four-square emphasis of:

❖ Christ the Savior
❖ Christ the baptizer in the Holy Spirit

❖ Christ the healer
❖ Christ the coming King

These biblical themes are woven throughout *The Apostolic Faith* newsletter published by W. J. Seymour from the Azusa Street Revival. The remarkable newsletters spanned the first two years of the revival from September 1906 through May 1908.

This devotional study guide may be used by individuals, groups, or classes. A leader's guide for group or class sessions is provided at the end of this devotional study for those using this guide in a group setting. Groups using this guide should complete their devotional studies prior to their group sessions, and greatly enhance sharing, studying, and praying together.

Individuals going through this guide can use it for daily devotional reading and study. The purpose of this guide is to help the reader(s) understand revival through the Scriptures with the insights from *The Apostolic Faith* newsletter. All of the insights quoted from that newletter are placed between lines and italicized for easy recognition. Each daily devotional study is structured to:

❖ Probe deeply into the Scriptures.
❖ Examine one's own personal relationship in faith with Jesus Christ.
❖ Discover biblical truths about revival.
❖ Encounter the person of Jesus Christ as personal Lord and Savior.

It is our prayer that as you study about revival daily in this devotional study, your personal walk with Christ will be renewed and revived by the power of the Holy Spirit.

Day 1

𝔗𝔥𝔢 𝔗𝔴𝔬 𝔚𝔬𝔯𝔨𝔰 𝔬𝔣 𝔊𝔯𝔞𝔠𝔢

Then Peter said unto them, Repent, and be baptized every one of you in the name of Jesus Christ for the remission of sins, and ye shall receive the gift of the Holy Ghost.

—ACTS 2:38

WE PREACH *old-time repentance, old-time conversion, old-time sanctification, and old-time baptism with the Holy Ghost, which is the gift of power upon the sanctified life; and God throws in the gift of tongues.*

Justification deals with our actual sins. When we go to God and repent, He washes all the guilt and pollution out of our hearts, and we stand justified like a new babe that never committed sin. We have no condemnation. If we walk in the Spirit, we can walk with Jesus and live a holy life before the Lord.

Prayer and repentance usher in revival. Prayer prepares the hearts of those who need to repent. Read what the following verses say about repentance and being justified by faith in Christ and write down what you discover:

Ezekiel 18:30 _____

_____

Matthew 4:17 _____

_____

Acts 2:38 _____

_____

Acts 3:19 _____

_____

Acts 17:30 _____

_____

2 Corinthians 7:9 _____

_____

Romans 5:1–2 _____

_____

Romans 5:16–18 _____

_____

ANCTIFICATION IS *the second and last work of grace. After we are justified, we have two battles to fight. There is sin inside and sin outside. There is warfare within, caused by past, inherited sin. When God brings the Word, "This is the will of God, even your sanctification" (1 Thess. 4:3), we should accept the Word. Then His blood comes and takes away all inherited sin. Everything is heavenly in you—you are a child of God. The Spirit of God witnesses in your heart that you are sanctified. The Spirit begins then and there leading us on to the baptism with the Holy Ghost.*

As a child of God, you should enter into the earnest of your inheritance. After you have a clear witness of the two works of grace in your heart, receive this gift of God, which is a free gift without repentance. Pray for the power of the Holy Ghost, and God will give you a new language.

To be *sanctified* means "to be set apart and made holy by the Holy Spirit." Read 2 Corinthians 7:1; 1 Thessalonians 4:3; and 1 Peter 3:15, and then summarize what you must do in sanctification: _____

_____

_____

_____

Now read the following verses, and summarize what Christ has done and is doing to sancitfy us (John 17:19; 1 Cor. 1:30; Eph. 6:26; 1 Thess. 5:23; 2 Thess. 2:13):

_____

_____

_____

Ask Yourself . . .

❖ Have you repented of all past sin?
❖ How is Christ sanctifying you now? How are you abstaining from all immorality?

If you have never repented of your sin and received Jesus as your Lord and Savior, pray:

Jesus, I repent of my sin and ask Your forgiveness through Your shed blood. I surrender to You and trust You as my Lord and Savior. I receive now the gift of Your Holy Spirit. Thank You for saving me. Amen.

If you have repented and accepted Christ, write a prayer thanking Him for justifying and sanctifying you:

_____

_____

_____

Day 2

I Know Thy Works

Nevertheless, I have somewhat against thee, because thou hast left thy first love.

—REVELATION 2:4

JESUS SAID THAT God *knows our works. He knows our hearts.* "*I know thy works, and thy labor, and thy patience, and how thou canst not bear them which are evil: and thou hast tried them which say they are apostles, and are not, and hast found them liars: and hast borne, and hast patience, and for my name's sake hast laboured, and hast not fainted*" (Rev. 2:2–3).

That Word is more than many churches today could receive from the Master. Jesus commended them for what they had done. He is not like men. He knows our hearts, trials, and conditions. Jesus does not make any allowance for sin. He hates sin today as much as He ever did. Yet He does not come to destroy us or condemn us, but to seek and to save us.

You are not under condemnation. Revival is not a move of the Spirit that condemns—but convicts (John 16:7–11). Read the following passages, and write down what they say about condemnation:

John 3:16–17 _____

_____

Romans 8:1–2 _____
_____

1 John 3:20–21 _____
_____

THE LORD DOES *not want anything to come between us and Him. May every precious child in these times that are getting the Holy Spirit not go into apostasy, but be a burning and a shining light for God, just as we were when we first received the baptism with the Holy Spirit. God wants us to keep the same anointing that we received and let nothing separate us from Christ.*

Jesus came to reconcile us to God and to break down any barrier separating us from Him. Read 2 Corinthians 5:19. Next to the wall below write anything that separates you from God.

_____
_____
_____
_____
_____
_____

Now pray, asking God to remove, through Christ's shed blood, any barrier between you and Him.

Day 2

The fire of revival is fueled by a passionate love for Jesus. Christ desires that you have a passionate, burning love for Him. How hot does your passion burn for Him? Put an *x* on the line that marks where you are now:

Passsionate for Jesus   Lukewarm   Cold

Ask Yourself. . .

❖ In what ways do you love Jesus more today than when you first met Him?

❖ What hinders you from being passionate for Jesus?

Write a prayer expressing your passionate love for Jesus:

Day 3

𝔗𝔥𝔢 𝔥𝔬𝔩𝔶 𝔊𝔥𝔬𝔰𝔱 𝔍𝔰 𝔓𝔬𝔴𝔢𝔯

*And my speech and my preaching was not with
enticing words of man's wisdom, but in demonstra-
tion of the Spirit and of power.*

—1 CORINTHIANS 2:4

HERE IS A *great difference between a sanctified person and one
who is baptized with the Holy Ghost and fire. A sanctified
person is cleansed and filled with divine love, but the one who is
baptized with the Holy Ghost has the power of God on his soul and
has power with God and men, power over all the kingdoms of Satan,
and over all his emissaries.*

*In all Jesus' great revivals and miracles, the work was wrought by
the power of the Holy Ghost flowing through His sanctified
humanity. When the Holy Ghost comes and takes us as His instru-
ments, this is the power that convicts men and women and causes
them to see that there is a reality in serving Jesus Christ.*

In revival, the power of the Holy Spirit is manifested.
How? Through the baptism of the Spirit, signs, wonders,
salvations, and miracles. Read the following passages
from Acts, and write down all the different ways you
observe the Spirit's moving in power:

Acts 2:1–7 _____

_____

Day 3

Acts 2:41–47

Acts 3:1–11

Acts 4:1–4

Acts 4:23–37

Acts 5:1–11

Acts 5:12–16

Acts 6:7–8

O H, BELOVED, *we ought to thank God that He has made us the tabernacles of the Holy Ghost. When you have the Holy Ghost, you have an empire, a power within yourself.*

The Lord never revoked the commission He gave to His disciples: "Heal the sick, cleanse the lepers, raise the dead . . . " (Matt. 10:8). Jesus is going to perform these things through us if He can get a people in unity.

Jesus said, "Behold, I give unto you power to tread on serpents and scorpions, and over all the powers of the enemy" (Luke 10:19).

What signs and wonders are you witnessing in your life and church? Has revival arrived, or is it still anticipated? Check all the evidences of the power of the Holy Spirit that you have witnessed recently in your life and church:

❑ Healings
❑ Miracles
❑ Deliverances
❑ Salvations
❑ Manifestations of the gifts
❑ The baptism of the Holy Spirit
❑ Signs and wonders
❑ Repentance
❑ Powerful prayer
❑ Other: _____

Ask Yourself . . .

❖ What will it take for revival to break out in your church?
❖ What will it take for revival to break out in you?

Write a prayer praying for revival in your life:

_____

_____

_____

Day 4

Continual Rebibal

Repent ye therefore, and be converted, that your sins may be blotted out, when the times of refreshing shall come from the presence of the Lord.

—ACTS 3:19

HE BAPTISM OF *the Spirit is the infilling of the personal Holy Ghost, which is the earnest of the Spirit. Then God gives us the authority to do the same work that Jesus did. Where men and women have received this baptism with the Spirit we find there is a revival going on, just as on the day of Pentecost. That is what the baptism of the Spirit means — continual revival.*

The baptism of the Holy Spirit brings both fire and power. The fire of the Holy Spirit purges, cleanses, and purifies us. Read the following passages about the Spirit's fire, and write down what each reveals about His fire:

Isaiah 43:14–16 _____

_____

Matthew 3:11–12 _____

_____

Luke 3:16–17 _____

_____

Acts 1:5,8; 2:1–4 _____

_____

1 Corinthians 3:12–15 _____

_____

1 Peter 1:7–9 _____

_____

The fire of the Holy Spirit burns away all the dross, wood, hay, and stubble from our lives (1 Cor. 3:12–15). On the flame below, write all the impurities now in your life that the baptizing fire of His Spirit needs to burn away:

The baptism of the Holy Spirit brings power. He empowers us to speak in tongues and pray in the Spirit (Acts 2). He empowers us with His gifts for witness and ministry (1 Cor. 12; Rom. 12; Eph. 4; 1 Pet. 4). The powerful baptism of the Holy Spirit ushers in Pentecost continually in our lives. Once we have encountered the Spirit's baptism our continual revival cry is, "More, Lord!" Our hunger and thirst for Him are continual. Our repentance and confession are constant. Our fellowship with Him is perpetual. And His power flows!

Shade the graph below to the level of your desire for *more* of His baptism in your life.

	More power!	*Some power!*	*Powerless*
Prayer			
Gifts			
Service			
Love			
Witness			

Ask Yourself . . .

❖ How is the Spirit's baptism of fire purifying you?

❖ Are you hungering and thirsting for more of His presence and power?

Write a prayer asking for more of the Spirit's baptism of fire and power in your life:

_____

_____

_____

Day 5

The Body of Christ

And whether one member suffer, all the members suffer with it; or one member be honored, all members rejoice with it. Now ye are the body of Christ.
—1 CORINTHIANS 12:26–27

IF YOU WANT *to see God work in power, see a people that are living in love, unity, and harmony. But if the devil can get in and divide the people of God and sow dissension among them, then God cannot work.*

Every blood-washed soul is a member of the body. We cannot reject one without hurting the whole body. All believers are important to the body of Christ.

Revival is both color-blind and classless because God is no respecter of persons (Acts 10:34). In revival, the Holy Spirit breaks down every wall of separation between people and unites them as one body in Christ. Read the following scriptures, and write down the unity in one body that we have in Christ:

Acts 2:1 _____

_____

1 Corinthians 3:1–11 _____

_____

1 Corinthians 12:12–31 _____

_____

Galatians 3:26–29 _____

_____

Ephesians 2:14–18 _____

_____

Ephesians 4:1–6 _____

_____

When God's Spirit is poured out in Pentecostal revival, all who seek Jesus are welcome regardless of background, race, or wealth. Examine yourself. If revival came, would you or your church have difficulty accepting anyone who came to Jesus? Remember the call of God is not, "Get right, and then come to Jesus." It's, "Come to Jesus, and He will make you righteous." Everyone is invited to revival's altar of repentance. Circle those against whom you or your church might be most prejudiced if they entered into the body:

The rich
The poor
Those of another race
Those of another denomination
Those dressed inappropriately
Those who are mentally or emotionally deficient
Those who are our critics
Those who smell and are unclean
Those who are divorced

Those who are immoral
Those who have committed heinous crimes
Other: _____

Ask Yourself . . .

❖ Do you have an unconditional love for the lost?
❖ Are you and your church willing to crucify your pride and pay the price for revival?

Write a prayer asking Jesus to give you love for the lost:

_____
_____
_____

Day 6

Praying for the Holy Ghost

*If ye then, being evil, know how to give good gifts
unto your children: how much more shall your heavenly Father give the Holy Spirit to them that ask him?*
—LUKE 11:13

WE ARE NOW *hearing from individuals and companies who are
definitely waiting on God for their personal Pentecost. Some
have been stimulated in seeking by hearing of God's visitation
in Los Angeles. We join hands with all such hungry seekers and meet
you at the throne.*

*Before another issue of this paper, we look for Brother Parham in
Los Angeles, a brother who is full of divine love and who the Lord
raised up five years ago to spread this truth. He, with other workers,
will hold union revival meetings in Los Angeles, and then expects to
go on to other towns and cities, and will appoint workers to fill the
calls that come in.*

Who is praying and working for revival in the land?
Without prayer, revival cannot come. Without working
the harvest, revival cannot come. Read 2 Chronicles 7:14
and Luke 10:2, and summarize what these verses teach
about prayer and harvest:

_____

_____

EGIN TO PRAY *right away for a revival in your neighborhood or town or city. Perhaps you need one in your own closet or at your family altar first. But expect great things from God. Begin to prepare for a revival—a great and deep revival—and believe for it. It may cost you money, and it may humble you, but prepare for the Lord's coming.*

What personal sacrifices are you willing to make to see revival come? Check each response that you are willing to make:

- ❏ Give money sacrificially and cheerfully.
- ❏ Pray without ceasing.
- ❏ Fast unto the Lord.
- ❏ Witness and work in the harvest.
- ❏ Serve the saints while they work in the harvest.
- ❏ Be trained and equipped to witness and disciple others.
- ❏ Other: _____

Revival is rooted in prayer, repentance, and a surrender that is willing to do whatever God asks.

Day 6

Ask Yourself . . .

❖   Are you willing to pay the cost of revival?
❖   If you are not willing, are you willing to let the
     Lord make you willing?

*Write a prayer seeking God to make you willing to pay the
cost of revival:*

_____

_____

_____

Day 7

Sanctification and Power

I pray not that thou shouldest take them out of the world, but that thou shouldest keep them from the evil. They are not of the world, even as I am not of the world.
—JOHN 17:15–16

HAVE YOU ACCEPTED *Jesus? Will you accept Him? Have you accepted Him as your sanctifier? "For this is the will of God, even your sanctification" (1 Thess. 4:3). Bless His dear name. He says, "Behold, I stand at the door, and knock: if any man hear my voice, and open the door, I will come in to him, and will sup with him, and he with me" (Rev. 3:20). Oh, let us invite Jesus into our hearts today that He might be our invited guest, and we shall sup with Him and He with us. Praises to our God. Hosanna to His omnipotent name!*

Jesus knocks at the door of your heart seeking to enter in. Will you open your heart and let Him enter in? Are there any locked doors in your heart? Are there hidden closets that you do not want Christ to open? On the doors on the following page, write the areas of your life that need to be fully opened to Christ [examples: finances, emotions, hurts, failures, insecurities, and so on]:

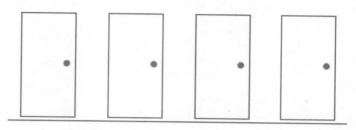

𝕴F WE ARE *sanctified and have clean hearts, living pure, holy lives, and having perfect love in our souls, oh, let us then receive the baptism with the Holy Ghost — the promise of the Father — that we may be able to be His witnesses in Jerusalem, Judea, and Samaria, and unto the uttermost parts of the earth. For Jesus gave this great commission in His resurrection power, after He rose from the dead. "Go ye therefore, and teach all nations, baptizing them in the name of the Father, and of the Son, and of the Holy Ghost: Teaching them to observe all things whatsoever I have commanded you: and, lo, I am with you always, even unto the end of the world" (Matt. 28:19–20).*

His great desire on the cross was for the salvation of souls.

Christ desires that you be in the great End-Time harvest of souls. Read the following passages, and write down His call upon your life:

Matthew 28:19–20 _____

_____

Mark 16:15–18 _____

_____

Luke 10:1–20 _____

_____

Acts 1:8 _____

_____

List those people around you who are lost and need to be saved. Commit yourself to pray for and witness to them:

_____

_____

_____

Ask Yourself . . .

❖ Are you witnessing to the lost, or expecting someone else to do that?

❖ Who have you recently led to Jesus?

Write a prayer opening your heart fully to Jesus:

_____

_____

_____

Day 8

Repentance

For godly sorrow worketh repentance to salvation not to be repented of: but the sorrow of the world worketh death.

—2 CORINTHIANS 7:10

WE FIND JESUS *still preaches the same doctrine of repentance that He preached while on earth.* "From that time Jesus began to preach, and to say, Repent: for the kingdom of heaven is at hand" (Matt. 4:17).

In order to get right with God, He says, "Remember therefore from whence thou art fallen, and repent, and do the first works; or else I will come unto thee quickly, and will remove thy candlestick out of his place, except thou repent" (Rev. 2:5).

To repent means to turn *from* sin and *to* Christ as Savior. For revival to be poured out by God's Spirit, the church needs to humble itself and cry out in repentance. When the world sees the church humbled before God, it will take notice of what Christ is doing. Revival begins in the church. What will it take for revival to break out in your church? Prioritize what needs to happen from the first step to the last:

_____ Witness to the lost.

_____ Repent of pride and self-centeredness.

_____ Pray and fast.

_____ Humble yourself before God.

_____ Be passionately in love with Jesus.

_____ Set aside human programs and ritual for Spirit-led ministry.

_____ Show evidence of a changed life, beginning with leadership.

F THERE IS *anything wrong in your life and Jesus has His finger upon it, oh, may you give it up, for Jesus is truly in His church today. This is the Holy Ghost dispensation, and He does convince men of sin, righteousness, and the judgment: If we will be honest, God will bless us.*

Turn to John 16:7–11. Write down the answers to the following questions:

Of what does the Spirit reprove or convict the world?

_____

_____

Why does He convict us? _____

_____

_____

What is the fate of Satan? _____

_____

Ask Yourself...

❖   What priority is revival in your church?
❖   Is your church willing to repent?

Write a prayer asking the conviction of the Holy Spirit to come upon your life:

_____

_____

_____

Day 9

Tarry in One Accord

And suddenly there came a sound from heaven as of a rushing mighty wind, and it filled all the house where they were sitting.

—ACTS 2:2

MAY EVERY CHILD *of God seek his personal Pentecost. We must stop quibbling and come to the standard that Jesus laid down for us. Wait on God for this baptism of the Holy Ghost just now.*

Gather two or three people together who are sanctified through the blood of Christ. Get into one accord, and God will send the baptism of the Holy Ghost upon your souls as the rain falls from heaven.

You may not have a preacher to come to you and preach the doctrine of the Holy Ghost and fire, but you can obey Jesus' saying in the passage, "For where two or three are gathered together in my name, there am I in the midst of them" (Matt. 18:20).

Revival involves meeting together in His presence and in unity. Without His presence there is no revival. When is Jesus in our midst? Read the following verses, and describe when He is present (Matt. 18:20, 28:16–20; Acts 2:1–2; John 14:16–17):

_____

_____

_____

THIS IS JESUS' *baptism—and if two or three gather together in His name and pray for the baptism of the Holy Ghost, they can have it this day or this night, because it is the promise of the Father. Glory to God!*

This was the Spirit that filled the house as a mighty rushing wind. The Holy Ghost is typified by wind, air, breath, life, and fire. "And there appeared unto them cloven tongues like as of fire, and it sat upon each of them. And they were all filled with the Holy Ghost, and began to speak with other tongues, as the Spirit gave them utterance" (Acts 2:3–4).

So, beloved, when you get your personal Pentecost, the signs will follow in speaking with tongues as the Spirit gives utterance. This is true. Wait on God and you will find it a truth in your own life. God's promises are true and sure.

Revival is a corporate as well as individual experience. It happens when *we* gather in His name. Revival fell on those gathered in unity under the name of Jesus as they waited for Pentecost. Once we repent and gather in love and unity, the Holy Spirit is free to move sovereignly in our midst. Complete these sentences:

When I pray with other believers, the Holy Spirit _____

_____.

When believers repent, God's response is _____

_____.

Our church will experience revival when _____

_____.

Ask Yourself . . .

❖ When do you gather with other believers in unity and love to pray for revival?

❖ How does Jesus manifest His presence in your midst?

Write a prayer asking for His presence to visit you when you gather with believers to seek Him:

_____

_____

_____

Day 10

The Baptism's Real Evidence

Though I speak with the tongues of men and of angels,
and have not charity, I am become as sounding brass,
or a tinkling cymbal.

—1 CORINTHIANS 13:1

THE REAL EVIDENCE *that a man or woman has received the baptism of the Holy Ghost is divine love, which is charity. That person will have the fruit of the Spirit.*

"But the fruit of the Spirit is love, joy, peace, longsuffering, gentleness, goodness, faith, meekness, temperance: against such there is no law. And they that are Christ's have crucified the flesh with the affections and lusts" (Gal. 5:22–24). The fruit of the Spirit is the real Bible evidence in our daily walk and conversation. The outward manifestations of the Spirit's baptism are speaking in tongues and signs following: casting out devils, laying hands on the sick and the sick being healed, and the love of God for souls increasing in our hearts (Mark 16:15–18).

The *fruit of the Spirit* is the character of Christ being formed in us, while the *gifts and manifestations of the Spirit* are the ministry of Christ as He works through us. Each piece of fruit in the fruit basket on the next page is labeled as one of the fruits of the Spirit. Shade each fruit to the level that it has matured and manifested in your life:

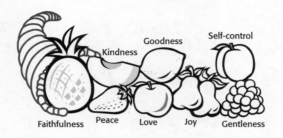

What outward manifestations of the fruit have you experienced in your own life or in your church? Circle all that you have experienced:

Casting out devils
Laying hands on the sick and seeing them healed
Speaking in tongues
Signs and wonders
Love for souls
Other: _____

Love is seeking God's best for another person. To whom do you need to demonstrate God's love today? List three people, and list how you will show them God's love:

Name   **I will love them by . . .**

_____   _____

_____   _____

_____   _____

_____   _____

Ask Yourself . . .

❖ How are you manifesting God's love?
❖ What fruits of the Spirit need most to mature in your life?

Write a prayer asking God to manifest both the nature and ministry of Christ through you:

_____

_____

_____

Day 11

The Polishing Process

But we all, with open face beholding as in a glass the glory of the Lord, are changed into the same image from glory to glory, even as by the Spirit of the Lord.
—2 CORINTHIANS 3:18

SEVERAL YEARS AGO *I shut myself away in my closet one day, and the Lord gave me a wonderful revelation. As I was kneeling before my Maker, beseeching Him to show me all He expected me to be, right before my eyes I saw this wonderful vision. There appeared a man with a large, long, knotty, but straight log. The man had an ax.*

He was scoring the log, and it seemed to me the ax went clear to the bit. And every time he scored, it hurt me. He scored it on four sides and then took the broad ax and whacked off the knots. Then he took a line and with an adz he made it pretty smooth. Then he raised it in the air, and taking a great plane, turned to me and said, "This is the plane of the Holy Ghost." He ran the plane up and down, until I could see the image of the man perfectly reflected in the face of the log, as in a mirror. He did this to all four sides. Then turning to me, he said: "Thou art all fair, my love; there is no spot in thee" (Song of Sol. 4:7).

That is what God wants to do with us. He wants to take all the bumps, all the barnacles off. We have only begun to lay ourselves on the anvil of God's truth. The hammer is being applied to us. He may have to throw us back in the smelter several times. Let us stay in the fire until there is no more dross in us. Let us stay on the anvil of God until we reflect the image of the Master.

God is transforming us by His Spirit into the image of Christ. The glorious result of that transformation is described in the Beatitudes. Each beatitude reflects a way God shapes us and a blessing that results. Read Matthew 5:1–12 and then put an *x* on the line that reflects where you are right now:

Poor in Spirit	Not aware of my spiritual lack
Brokenhearted by what breaks God's heart	Not saddened by hurt and sin
Humble	Proud
Hungering and thirsting for righteousness	Self-righteous
Merciful	Unforgiving
Pure in heart	Impure heart
Peacemaker	Angry
Persecuted for righteousness' sake	Unwilling to make waves

Look over your list and determine which area needs the most growth right now in your life.

Ask Yourself . . .

❖　Are you being polished by Christ?
❖　Do you desire to grow in every way possible?

Write a prayer asking Jesus to polish whatever area of your life needs it for His glory:

_____

_____

_____

Day 12

Back to Pentecost

For thus saith the Lord God; Behold, I, even I, will both search my sheep, and seek them out.
—EZEKIEL 34:11

HAT IS THE *meaning of these salaried preachers over the land that will not preach unless they get so much salary? People have wandered from the old landmarks. The priests had no land of their own. They were to live on the tithes and offerings. The ministers of today have wandered from the old landmarks. Therefore they are seeking salary over the land. Get back. You have no time to lose.*

Do you want to be blessed? Do you want the approbation of God? Be a servant to humanity. The loaves and fishes did not multiply in the hands of our blessed Redeemer until He began to give out to the hungry. God does not need a great theological preacher that can give nothing but theological chips and shavings to people. He takes the weak things to confound the mighty. He can pick up a worm and thrash a mountain. He is picking up pebble stones from the street and polishing them for His work. He is using even the children to preach His gospel.

God can use anyone to declare His message of repentance and new life for revival. He wants us to have faith as a little child so that we can receive and share His good news. Read the following verses about becoming a child in faith, and write down what you discover:

Matthew 18:1–5 _____

_____

Mark 10:15 _____

_____

Luke 9:47–48 _____

_____

Luke 18:16 _____

_____

A YOUNG SISTER, *fourteen years old, was saved, sanctified, and baptized with the Holy Ghost and went out, taking a band of workers with her, and led a revival in which one hundred ninety souls were saved. Salaried ministers that are rejecting the gospel will have to go out of business. He is sending out those who will go without money and without price.*

Revival and God's power cannot be bought. No one profits financially from revival. In Luke Jesus sends out the seventy-two to proclaim the gospel. Read Luke 10:1–16, and complete the following statements:

Those who go out are not to take _____

_____.

When they go into a home, they must _____

_____.

Day 12

When entering a town, those following Jesus should _____

_____.

Those who reject the proclamation of the Good News will _____

_____.

Not everyone welcomes revival. But we are still called to go and proclaim Good News.

Ask Yourself . . .

❖   What keeps you from sharing the Good News of Christ?

❖   Are you seeking any reward from sharing the Good News?

Write a prayer asking Christ to give you faith as a little child and to send you wherever He wishes you to go:

_____

_____

_____

Day 13

The Baptism of a Clean Heart

*And Jesus being full of the Holy Ghost returned from
Jordan, and was led by the Spirit into the wilderness.*
—LUKE 4:1

---

*J*ESUS IS OUR *example. Upon His clean heart, the baptism fell. We
find in reading the Bible that the baptism with the Holy Ghost and
fire falls on a clean, sanctified life. For we see, according to the
Scriptures, that Jesus was filled with wisdom and favor with God and
man before God anointed Him with the Holy Ghost and power. For in
Luke 2:40, we read, "[Jesus] waxed strong in spirit, filled with wisdom:
and the grace of God was upon him." Then in Luke 2:52, "And Jesus
increased in wisdom and stature, and in favor with God and man."*

*After Jesus was empowered with the Holy Ghost at Jordan, He
returned in the power of the Spirit into Galilee, and there went out a
fame of Him through all the region round about. He was not any
more holy or any more meek, but had greater authority. "And he
taught in their synagogues, being glorified by all" (Luke 4:15).*

*Beloved, if Jesus, who was God Himself, needed the Holy Ghost
to empower Him for His ministry and His miracles, how much more
do we children need the Holy Ghost baptism today. Oh that men and
women would tarry for the baptism with the Holy Ghost and fire
upon their souls!*

Jesus was empowered by the Holy Spirit for ministry.
Below is a list of the ways He was empowered in Luke's
Gospel by the Spirit. Match the correct verse with each
empowerment by drawing a line from one to the other:

Jesus was . . .	Found in . . .
Conceived by the Spirit	Luke 4:14
Descended upon by the Spirit	Luke 3:21
Filled with the Spirit	Luke 1:35
Led by the Spirit	Luke 10:21
Empowered by the Spirit	Luke 4:1
Anointed by the Spirit	Luke 4:18
Filled with the Spirit's joy	Luke 4:1

Now look at the different ways Jesus was empowered by the Holy Spirit, and underline all the empowerments you have experienced in your Christian walk.

Ask Yourself . . .

❖ Are you doing anything in your life to hinder the Spirit?

❖ How do you desire the Spirit to touch your life now?

Write a prayer asking Jesus to baptize you with the full anointing and power of the Holy Spirit:

_____

_____

_____

Day 14

A Pure and Holy Life

For both he that sanctifieth and they who are sancti-
fied are all of one: for which cause he is not ashamed
to call them brethren.

—HEBREWS 2:11

IN ORDER TO *live a pure and holy life one does not need the*
baptism of the Holy Ghost. The Holy Ghost does not cleanse
anyone from sin. It is Jesus' shed blood on Calvary that cleanses
us from sin. The Holy Ghost never died for our sins. It was Jesus who
died for our sins, and it is His blood that atones.

"If we walk in the light, as he is in the light, we have fellowship one
with another, and the blood of Jesus Christ his Son cleanseth us from
all sin.... If we confess our sins, he is faithful and just to forgive us our
sins, and to cleanse us from all unrighteousness" (1 John 1:7, 9). It is
the blood that cleanses and makes holy, and through the blood we
receive the baptism of the Holy Spirit. The Holy Ghost always falls in
response to the blood.

The blood of Jesus Christ cleanses and purifies us
while opening the door to the Spirit of God and revival.
The effective power of His blood paves the way for personal forgiveness and renewal. Read these passages about
the blood, and jot down what each says about the power
of the blood to affect your life:

John 6:55–56

Romans 3:25, 5:9

Ephesians 1:7, 2:13

Colossians 1:14–20

Hebrews 9:20–25

Hebrews 13:12–20

1 Peter 1:17–20

1 John 1:7–9

Meditate on the blood of Christ. He is the Passover Lamb whose blood was shed for us (Exod. 12; 1 Pet. 1:19). Revival can start right in your own family. On the next page is a doorpost with the blood applied to the sidepost and the top. On the cross in the center, write the name of each family member who is covered by the saving blood of Jesus.

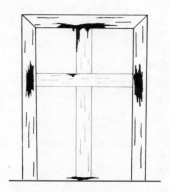

Ask Yourself . . .

❖ Is everyone in your family covered by the blood of Christ?

❖ If some are not, are you praying for their salvation?

Write a prayer covering all of your unsaved family members with the blood of Christ and seeking God for their salvation:

_____

_____

_____

Day 15

We Must Humble Ourselves

*Whosoever therefore shall humble himself as this little
child, the same is greatest in the kingdom of heaven.*
—MATTHEW 18:4

SOME SAY THAT *it takes little "thimble-brained" people to accept
this gospel. We have so much unbelief that we must be emptied
out before we can be filled. The one that does not know any
more than just to believe God, gets down and takes Him at His Word,
and the witness comes that the blood of Jesus does save and sanctify
from all sin. In faith the believer trusts the promises of the Father,
receives the baptism of the Holy Spirit, and receives the Bible evidence of that. It is now, as in the time of Christ, when the people
heard Him gladly.*

Those who have been revived trust the promises of
God. His promises are true yesterday, today, and forever.
It is impossible to have revival among those who cannot
trust His promises. Read the following verses about His
promises, and complete the sentences (Rom. 15:8; 2
Cor. 1:20; 2 Cor. 7:1; 2 Pet. 1:4; 1 John 2:25):

God has promised us _____

_____ .

God reveals His faithfulness when He _____

_____ .

When we take God at His promise, we experience ____

_____ .

God's promise that means the most to me is _____

_____ .

───────────────────────────────────────

𝕋HE GREEKS *required knowledge and the Jews a sign, but the simple-hearted people just believed Jesus. The Lord has such people today that are following the Lamb whithersoever He goeth.*

May God help us to humble ourselves to receive all that the Holy Ghost has for us.

───────────────────────────────────────

What keeps you from completely trusting the promises of God? Do you need a sign or special knowledge, or is God's Word enough for you? Check all the things that you believe are necessary in order to confirm His Word:

❏ Special signs and wonders
❏ A personal word of wisdom or knowledge
❏ A fleece that has been fulfilled
❏ A multitude of witnesses and confirmations
❏ Other: _____

Ask Yourself...

❖ What are you expecting God to do to bring revival?

❖ What is God expecting of you in order for His revival to be released?

Write a prayer asking God to inspire you with simple faith to trust His promises:

_____

_____

_____

Day 16

Contend for the Faith

Beloved, [I] exhort you that ye should earnestly contend for the faith which was once delivered unto the saints.

—JUDE 1:3

IT IS OUR *privilege to contend earnestly for the power that was in the early apostolic church — so that men will be instantly healed and baptized with the Holy Ghost. The power of God is going to fall on men in our cities. God wants people who will believe in Him and exercise faith. Faith moves God. Faith is one thing that gets results with God (Heb. 11).*

The only substance God needs for creating revival is faith. God uses our faith to implement His will and way in our lives, just as He uses us to ignite revival. Read these passages, and list at least five things that faith is and does (Matt. 9:22, 17:20; Luke 7:50; Rom. 5:1–2, 10:9; 2 Cor. 1:24; Gal. 2:16; Eph. 3:17; 2 Thess. 1:11; Heb. 11:6, 12:1–2; James 2:14–20):

1. _____

2. _____

3. _____

4. _____

5. _____

W̲HEN THEY PUT *Paul and Silas in the Philippian jail, they went joyfully (Acts 16). They sang and prayed, and at midnight God heard their prayers in heaven and shook the earth until the* doors flew open. The jailer trembled and was going to take his life. But he fell under conviction. What happened? All were saved.

When those men called upon God, something happened. I believe those men had faith in God. When are we going to get that perfect faith? The Lord is just preparing His people now for the work He is going to do. We have been a great distance from His work. The devil does not like to see us victorious, but Satan has already been defeated by God. Believers who contend for the faith are overcomers. They are more than conquerors in Christ Jesus.

Faith delivers us from the enemy's bondage. Read the story of Paul and Silas' release from prison in Acts 16, and then answer the following questions:

What attitudes did Paul and Silas exhibit in prison? ____

_____

How did they treat the Philippian jailor? ____

_____

What brought revival to the jailor's household? ____

_____

Revival can come out of hardship and suffering. Just because you face difficult circumstances, do not give up. Walk in faith, and trust God to use you as an instrument of salvation in the lives of others.

Ask Yourself . . .

❖ Do you expect revival when circumstances are difficult?

❖ Do you want God to change your circumstances or to use your circumstances to bring you and those around you to Christ?

Write a prayer asking God to use your circumstances for His glory:

_____

_____

_____

Day 17

Healing

Is any sick among you? let him call for the elders of the church; and let them pray over him, anointing him with oil in the name of the Lord.

—JAMES 5:14

JESUS STILL HEALS *today. Praise God! Jesus said, "Men ought always to pray, and not to faint" (Luke 18:1). Many precious children of God today, instead of praying, commence grieving. But God's Word says, "Let him pray." And if we obey His Word, He will heal us. We read in Psalm 107:20, "He sent his word, and healed them, and delivered them from their destructions." And we read in Proverbs 4:20, "My son, attend to my words; incline thine ear unto my sayings."*

Jesus is speaking through the power of the Holy Ghost to every believer to keep His precious Word. "Let them not depart from thine eyes; keep them in the midst of thine heart. For they are life unto those that find them, and health to all their flesh" (Prov. 4:21–22).

One manifestation of the Spirit's moving in revival is healing. God heals, delivers, saves, and sets us free when He moves in power. Write down what the Word reveals about His healing:

Exodus 15:26 _____

_____

Psalm 103:3 _____

Psalm 107:20 _____

Jeremiah 17:14 _____

Mark 6:13 _____

James 5:14–15 _____

_____

E READ IN *Exodus 15:26, "I am the Lord that healeth thee." Jesus said, "And as Moses lifted up the serpent in the wilderness, even so must the Son of man be lifted up: That whosoever believeth in him should not perish, but have eternal life"* (John 3:14–15).

Dear beloved, we see in receiving the words of Jesus, it brings not only life to our souls and spirits but to these physical bodies. For His words are medicine to our bodies through faith.

God revives us physically, emotionally, mentally, and spiritually with His healing power. Do you need His healing? Complete the following sentences:

I need His physical healing for _____

_____.

Day 17

I need His emotional healing for _____

_____ .

I need His intellectual healing for _____

_____ .

I need His spiritual healing for _____

_____ .

Ask Yourself . . .

- ❖ Are you praising God for your healing before you see it?
- ❖ Are you willing to allow God to use you as an instrument?

Write a prayer asking God to heal you completely:

_____

_____

_____

Day 18

Pure Channels

Draw nigh to God, and he will draw nigh to you. Cleanse your hands, ye sinners; and purify your hearts, ye double-minded.

—JAMES 4:8

I F MEN AND *women today will consecrate themselves to God— their hands and feet and eyes and affections, body and soul, all sanctified—how the Holy Ghost will use such people.*

He will find pure channels to flow through, sanctified avenues for His power. People will be saved, sanctified, healed, and baptized with the Holy Ghost and fire.

The Holy Spirit desires to sanctify us totally—body, soul, and spirit. Read 1 Thessalonians 5:23. In the three circles below labeled *body, soul,* and *spirit,* shade each circle to the degree that area of your life has been sanctified by the Holy Spirit.

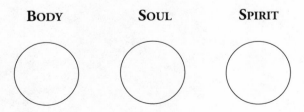

BODY   **SOUL**   **SPIRIT**

Day 18

HE BAPTISM OF *the Holy Ghost comes through our Lord and Savior Jesus Christ by faith in His Word. In order to receive it, we must first be sanctified. Then we can become His witnesses unto the uttermost parts of the earth.*

You will never have an experience to measure with Acts 2:4 and Acts 2:16–17 until you get your personal Pentecost for the baptism with the Holy Ghost and fire (Matt. 3:11).

This is the latter rain that God is pouring out upon His humble children in the last days. We are preaching a gospel that measures with the great commission that Jesus gave His disciples when He arose from the dead (Matt. 28:19–20). They received the power to implement this commission on the day of Pentecost (Acts 2:4). Bless the Lord. Oh, how I bless God to see His mighty power manifested in these last days. God wants His people to receive the baptism with the Holy Ghost and fire.

Your personal Pentecost and revival includes your own encounter with the Holy Spirit. Describe how the Holy Spirit is sanctifying your life now:

_____

_____

_____

Ask Yourself . . .

❖   Where in your life do you most need sanctification?

❖   Where do you experience the most power in your life?

Write a prayer asking God's Spirit to sanctify you—body, soul, and spirit:

_____

_____

_____

Day 19

Love

And now abideth faith, hope, charity, these three; but the greatest of these is charity.

—1 CORINTHIANS 13:13

IT IS SWEET TO *have the promise of Jesus and the character of Jesus wrought out in our lives and hearts by the power of the blood and the Holy Ghost, and to have that same love and that same meekness. Jesus was a man of love — the love of God incarnate in a body.*

Is God's love at work in your life? Below is the New Living Translation's version of 1 Corinthians 13:4–8. As you read, underline the qualities of love that are strongest in your life, and circle the qualities that are weakest.

GOD'S LOVE AT WORK IN YOU . . .

Love is patient and kind. Love is not jealous or boastful or proud or rude. Love does not demand its own way. Love is not irritable, and it keeps no record of when it has been wronged. It is never glad about injustice but rejoices whenever the truth wins out. Love never gives up, never loses faith, is always hopeful, and endures through every circumstance. Love will last forever, but prophecy and speaking in unknown languages and special knowledge will all disappear.

We must have that pure love that comes down from heaven. Such love is willing to suffer loss, not puffed up, not easily provoked, but gentle, meek, and humble. We are accounted as sheep for the slaughter day by day. We are crucified to self, the world, the flesh, and everything, that we may bear about in our body the dying of the Lord Jesus so that our joy may be full even as He is full.

If revival is to ignite our lives and churches, then God's love for others must first ignite us. He gives us an unconditional love for the lost. Like the Lord, we passionately desire for the lost to be saved.

Examine the love in your life. From the list below, place a checkmark by each group it is difficult for you to love:

❏ Family members or relatives
❏ Those of a different ethnic group or economic class
❏ People from a different religion
❏ Enemies
❏ Strangers
❏ Church members
❏ Those who have hurt me
❏ Others: _____

Ask Yourself . . .

❖ Do I love the lost with God's love?
❖ With whom am I sharing the gospel today?

Write a prayer asking God to give you His love for the lost:

_____

_____

_____

Day 20

The Spirit Follows the Blood

And such were some of you: but ye are washed, but ye are sanctified, but ye are justified in the name of the Lord Jesus, and by the Spirit of our God.
—1 CORINTHIANS 6:11

JESUS SAID, "Now ye are clean through the word which I have spoken unto you" (John 15:3). That cleansing took place before the Pentecostal baptism. Jesus said on that night before He was betrayed, "Ye are not all clean" (John 13:11). Jesus knew that Judas had the devil in him.

The disciples had been sanctified before Pentecost, for the Word of God is true. We know they had been justified a long time before, for He said, "Rejoice not, that the spirits are subject unto you; but rather rejoice, because your names are written in heaven" (Luke 10:20). And we know they were sanctified when Jesus prayed for them, for Jesus' prayers did not have to be answered in the future but were answered in the present. He said, "They are not of the world, even as I am not of the world" (John 17:16).

They were not only sanctified but had received the Holy Spirit in a certain measure, because He breathed on them in the upper room and said, "Receive ye the Holy Ghost" (John 20:22).

The heart must be clean before the Holy Ghost can endue with power from on high. It is not the work of the Holy Ghost to burn up inherited sin and carnality. He is not our Savior. It is the blood that cleanses us from all sin. The disciples were cleansed and sanctified and were sitting and waiting when the Holy Ghost fell upon them.

God instructs us to be children of light—not children of the dark. Picture a dirty window. It is difficult for light to shine through. Our lives are windows to God. His light shines through the cleansed panes of our lives. In each window pane below there is a scripture. Read that scripture, then blacken the window pane to the degree His light is not shining through in that area of witness in your life. For example, Matthew 25:31–45 talks about witnessing to the "least of these" by serving them. If you rarely do this, then shade most of the window pane.

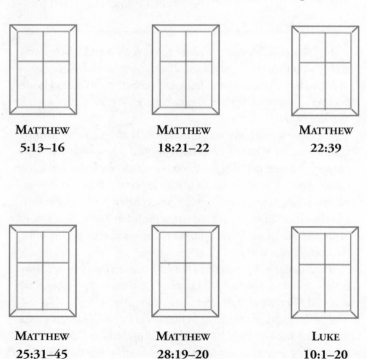

| MATTHEW 5:13–16 | MATTHEW 18:21–22 | MATTHEW 22:39 |
| MATTHEW 25:31–45 | MATTHEW 28:19–20 | LUKE 10:1–20 |

Day 20

Ask Yourself . . .

❖   Are your light and witness for Christ shining brightly for others to see?
❖   How is God cleansing your life right now?

Write a prayer asking God to cleanse and then shine through every area of your life:

_____

_____

_____

Day 21

Sanctification

For this is the will of God, even your sanctification.
— 1 THESSALONIANS 4:3

THERE IS NOTHING *sweeter, higher, or holier in this world than sanctification. The baptism with the Holy Ghost is the gift of power upon the sanctified soul, giving power to preach the gospel of Christ and power to go to the stake. It seals you unto the day of redemption, that you may be ready to meet the Lord Jesus at midnight or any time, because you have oil in your vessel with your lamp.*

Are you wisely and alertly waiting on the bridegroom, or are you foolish? Put another way: Are you ready for the outpouring oil of His Spirit in revival? If Jesus arrived while you worshiped or prayed for revival at church, would He be recognized or welcomed? Are you or your church really ready for revival?

Read Matthew 25:1–13. Then answer the following questions:

Which virgins loved Jesus? _____

_____

Why were the foolish virgins not ready? _____

_____

Are you ready for Jesus whenever He comes? _____

_____

How have you prepared for revival in your own life? ____

_____

In what ways is your church prepared for revival? _____

_____

> OU ARE PARTAKER *of the Holy Ghost in the Pentecostal baptism, just as you were partaker of the Lord Jesus Christ in sanctification. You become partaker of the eternal Spirit of God in the baptism with the Holy Ghost.*
>
> *Jesus was God's Son before He received the baptism, sanctification, and was sent into the world, but yet He could not go on His great mission fighting against the combined forces of hell until He received the baptism with the Holy Ghost. If He needed it, how much more we as His servants ought to get the same thing.*

An important way to be prepared for Jesus' arrival is by being baptized with the fire and power of the Holy Spirit (Acts 1–2; Matt. 3:11–12). How has the baptism of the Holy Spirit prepared you for revival? In what ways are you unprepared? Complete the following sentences:

I am prepared for Jesus to bring revival because _____

_____ .

The baptism of the Spirit has made me ready for revival by _____

_____ .

Ask Yourself . . .

❖ If Jesus poured out revival-fire with His presence right now on your life or your church, would you be ready?

❖ How are you staying prepared for revival?

Write a prayer asking Jesus to teach you how to stay prepared for His coming, whenever and however He chooses to come:

_____

_____

_____

_____

Day 22

Crucified With Christ

I am crucified with Christ: nevertheless I live; yet not I, but Christ liveth in me: and the life which I now live in the flesh I live by the faith of the Son of God.
—GALATIANS 2:20

JESUS IS SEARCHING *for a people who will believe the gospel. He has never changed the gospel in any way since He commissioned it. Many take sanctification to be the power. They stop when they have the original sin taken out and Christ has been enthroned on their hearts. But God wants us to go on to be filled with the Holy Ghost that we may be witnesses unto Him to the uttermost parts of the earth.*

The times of ignorance God winked at, but now He commands men everywhere to repent. The Lord is restoring all the gifts to His church. He wants people everywhere to repent. He wants a people who have faith in His Word and in the Holy Spirit.

Jesus was not only nailed to the cross, but hung there until He died. He did not come down from the cross as they told Him to do, though He had the power to do so. So with us, when we are crucified with Christ, we should not come down and live for self again, but stay on the cross. A constant death to self is the way to follow our Master.

Until we die to self, revival will never come in our lives or church. Scripture is filled with revelation about dying to selfishness, pride, and self-centeredness. Read the following verses, and write down what they say about dying to self:

2 Chronicles 7:14 _____

_____

Psalm 51:1–19 _____

_____

Matthew 10:39–42 _____

_____

Matthew 16:25–26 _____

_____

Luke 9:24–25 _____

_____

Luke 17:33 _____

_____

Romans 12:1–2 _____

_____

Galatians 2:20 _____

_____

Philippians 2:1–11 _____

_____

Philippians 3:7–9 _____

_____

Have you truly died to self? If not, why not? What keeps you holding on to sin and the past? Check all that apply to you:

- ❏ Fear of losing control
- ❏ Unbelief
- ❏ Desire to continue in past sin
- ❏ Unconfessed sin
- ❏ Ignorance
- ❏ Other: _____

If you have not surrendered all to Christ, then do so now so that He can pour His revival fire into your life and ignite you with passionate love for Him.

Ask Yourself . . .

- ❖ What will it take for you to surrender all?
- ❖ In what ways do you need to die to self today?

Write a prayer expressing how you will die to self:

_____

_____

_____

Day 23

Spread the Fire

For by one Spirit are we all baptized into one body,
whether we be Jews or Gentiles, whether we be bond or
free; and have been all made to drink into one Spirit.
—1 CORINTHIANS 12:13

WHEN BROTHER William Pendleton and thirty-five of his
members were turned out of the Holiness church, they were
invited by Brother Bartleman and other workers to occupy the
church at Eighth Street and Maple Avenue. It had just been opened
up for Pentecostal work. And God has been using them as never
before.

When some of the saints were rejected from the Nazarene church
at Elysian Heights on account of the baptism with the Holy Ghost
and evidence of tongues, they opened cottage prayer meetings where
hungry souls flocked.

Truth crushed to earth will rise again.

The eternal years of God are hers;

But error wounded writhes in pain,

And dies among its worshipers.

Are you hungry and thirsty for God? Have you been
in a wilderness or famine experience where you feel
starved for the presence of Jesus and are thirsty for His
living waters? Read John 6:35 and 48. Then, near the
bread on the next page, write all that you hunger and
thirst for from Jesus, your bread of life.

IN CALIFORNIA *where there has been no unity among churches, they are becoming one against this Pentecostal movement. But, thank God, the source is from the skies and cannot be cut off from below. The dear church people know not what they do. Many of them are hungry, and coming and saying, "This is just what I have been longing for, for years."*

God is drawing His people together and making them one. No new church or division of the body of Christ is being formed. Christ never had but one church. We may be turned out of the big wood and brick structures, but "by one Spirit are we all baptized into one body" (1 Cor. 12:13).

Pentecost came when the first followers and disciples of Jesus were meeting together in *one accord*—unity. How unified is the body of Christ where you worship? How unified is the body in your town or city? Put an *x* on the line to represent your church and community's position:

In our church we are

_____

Unified   Divided

In our town, Christians are

_____

Unified   Divided

One thing I need to do to bring more unity to the body
of Christ is _____

_____ .

Ask Yourself . . .

- ❖ Are you praying, serving, worshiping, and
  loving other believers in your church and
  town?
- ❖ How are churches working together to win the
  lost where you live?

*Write a prayer for unity among believers in the body of
Christ:*

_____

_____

_____

Day 24

The True Pentecost

Greater is he that prophesieth than he that speaketh with tongues.

—1 CORINTHIANS 14:5

WE CAN HAVE *all the nine gifts as well as the nine fruits of the Spirit, for in Christ Jesus dwells all the fullness of the Godhead bodily.* Paul is simply teaching the church to be in unity and not to be confused because all have not the same gifts.

We are not confused because one has his Pentecost and another has not been sanctified. We do not say that we do not need the justified or the sanctified brother simply because he does not speak with tongues or does not prophesy. But we realize that it takes the justified, the sanctified, and the Pentecost brother all to make up the body of Christ.

You may have the gift of wisdom, healing, or prophecy, but when you get the Pentecost, the Lord God will speak through you in tongues.

"Greater is he that prophesieth than he that speaketh with tongues, except he interpret." The brother that prophesies is no greater than the brother that speaks in tongues if the brother interprets as he speaks. We have a good many here that interpret as they speak, and it is edifying. The gifts are for you if you will only ask the Lord for them.

Below is a list of the gifts of the Spirit. Place a checkmark beside the gifts that you see manifested in your church now. Circle the gifts that you are praying will

69

come into your church in order for full ministry to occur among the saints.

❏ Wisdom   ❏ Knowledge
❏ Faith   ❏ Healing
❏ Prophecy   ❏ Discernment
❏ Tongues   ❏ Interpret tongues
  (unknown languages)   (unknown languages)
❏ Miracles   ❏ Teaching
❏ Helping others   ❏ Apostle
❏ Serving others   ❏ Encouraging
❏ Ability to lead   ❏ Giving generously
❏ Kindness   ❏ Evangelism
❏ Pastoring   ❏ Preaching

IN 1 CORINTHIANS 14, *Paul is setting in order those who have the baptism with the Holy Ghost and the speaking in tongues, that we should not get puffed up. In getting into deep spiritual things and into the hidden mysteries of God, people have to keep very humble at the feet of the Lord Jesus, for these precious gifts can easily puff us up if we do not keep under the blood.*

We should never take pride in revival or renewal. Both are a gift of grace and never come because we deserve them, only because God gives us revival out of His mercy and love for us. Complete the following sentences:

I praise God for stirring these gifts up in me: _____

_____.

Day 24

I am tempted to become prideful when God gifts me to

_____.

One way I resist pride when ministering in the gifts is

_____.

Ask Yourself . . .

❖ Are you remaining humble before the Lord?
❖ When others minister with gifts you have not operated in, how do you feel?

Write a prayer praising God for His mercy in giving you gifts of the Spirit for ministry:

_____

_____

_____

Day 25

Cured of Doubt and Fear

For God hath not given us the spirit of fear; but of power, and of love, and of a sound mind.
—2 TIMOTHY 1:7

THE BLOOD OF *Jesus is the only cure for doubt and fear. It takes sanctification to deliver a person from doubt and fear. We always find that people who are not sanctified are more or less troubled with doubt. But when they get sanctified they are filled with such love to God that they are like little babes, they believe every word of Jesus.*

Jesus had been with the disciples three-and-a-half years, and had told them all about the kingdom, and yet the doubts and fears came upon them. But in Luke 24:31 we read, "And their eyes were opened, and they knew him." After the Resurrection their spiritual eyes were opened to know Jesus.

Our eyes must be opened to see our inheritance. No one can get the baptism until Christ anoints his eyes and opens up his understanding that he might understand the Scriptures. "Then opened he their understanding, that they might understand the scriptures" (Luke 24:45). Then they received the living Word into their hearts, and their hearts burned within them as He unfolded the Scriptures to them.

We have nothing to fear, nothing to hide, and nothing to lose in following Jesus Christ. In Him are courage, truth, and abundance. List those things you used to fear but now do not fear:

Because of Jesus, I no longer fear _____

_____.

Because of Jesus, I no longer hide _____

_____.

Because of Jesus, I cannot lose _____

_____.

ANCTIFICATION IS A *cure for unbelief, doubts, and fears. Jesus got all His disciples cured before He went back to glory. What do you call that but sanctification?*

We can see that Jesus taught the doctrine of sanctification before He was crucified, for He had prayed that they might be sanctified in John 17. He stayed with them on earth forty days, opened their understanding, opened their eyes, and cleansed them of doubt.

Read the New Living Translation's version of John 17:1–10. Complete each of the following sentences by inserting your own name in the blanks:

17:6   "I have told _____ about you. _____ was in the world, but then you gave _____ to me."

17:7   "Now _____ know[s] that everything I have is a gift from you."

17:8   "I have passed on to _____ the words that you gave me; and _____ accepted them and know[s] that I came from you, and _____ believe[s] you sent me."

17:9   "My prayer is not for the world, but for
_____ . . . because _____ belong[s]
to you."

17:10 "And . . . _____ belong[s] to you, and you
have given _____ back to me, so
_____ [is] my glory."

The same sanctifying prayer that Jesus prayed over His
disciples is the one He prays over you. You are sanctified
by His Word. Rejoice in your sanctification.

Ask Yourself . . .

❖   Are you walking in the sanctification of His
Spirit in your life?
❖   How is your sanctification bringing revival to
your family and church?

*Write a prayer thanking Jesus for sanctifying you by His
Spirit and Word:*

_____

_____

_____

Day 26

Pray Through

The effectual fervent prayer of a righteous man availeth much.

—JAMES 5:16

WE OUGHT NOT *to stop until we pray through and receive our requests from God. We should prevail with God until we get a witness. Elijah prayed for rain and sent his servant seven times until he got the witness, which was a cloud the size of a man's hand. Then Elijah arose and went to tell Ahab that the rain was coming (1 Kings 18:42–44).*

Paul prayed thrice for a certain thing before God answered him (2 Cor. 12:8). God heard the first time, but Paul did not get the answer until he had prayed three times.

Oh, we should press or claim before the throne until we receive a witness by the power of the Holy Ghost. God will do just what He promises.

Do you persist and persevere in prayer? Put an *x* on the line that represents where you are right now:

I pray

Sporadically   Through

When things are tough I

_____

Wait on God   Panic

In seeking God, I

_____

Talk and listen   Talk and leave

Read James 5:16–18. What does it reveal to you about how you need to be praying for revival? Answer these questions *yes* or *no*.

Are you praying for revival in your life? _____

Are you praying for revival in your church? _____

Are you praying for revival in the body of Christ? _____

Will you continue praying for revival until revival is poured out from heaven? _____

Ask Yourself . . .

❖   Are you willing to pray through for revival?
❖   What makes you impatient? Will you surrender that to God?

Write a prayer asking God to strengthen you with perseverance in prayer:

_____

_____

_____

Day 27

Traditions and Dead Forms

Making the word of God of none effect through your tradition, which ye have delivered: and many such like things do ye.

—MARK 7:13

OH, IT IS *easy to follow the Spirit of God if you have been born of the Spirit. And it is easy to manifest the Spirit if the Spirit of God is within you. It is impossible for both good and impure water to come from the same spring. Just as surely as the blood of Jesus Christ has been applied to the soul, you will not only know it, but your neighbors will know it. And those working with you will know it.*

It means so much to have the blood of Jesus Christ applied to your soul. Dead forms and ceremonies are done away, and every sin must be washed away by the blood of Jesus.

It is not tomorrow in sin and today out of sin, but if the blood of Jesus has atoned for you, it has atoned for today and tomorrow — once and for all.

Have you been washed in the blood of Jesus and born of the Spirit? If so, do you know how to share with the lost how to be saved? Read John 3, Romans 3:23, 5:8, 8:1, 10:9, 13; and Acts 2:38. Then complete the following sentences in such a way that any unsaved person could understand the gospel:

I trust Jesus because _____

_____.

Without Jesus we are sinners because _____

_____.

God loves us and gave Jesus to die for us because ____

_____.

To be saved, we must _____

_____.

If every Christian in your church witnessed to one lost person each day, then the preparation for revival would be laid in your church.

Ask Yourself . . .

❖ Are you witnessing to the lost regularly? Is your church?

❖ What needs to be done to ignite evangelism in you and your church?

Pray that God fills you with compassion and boldness to witness to the lost.

Day 28

Beginning of Worldwide Revival

I dwell in the high and holy place, with him also that is
of a contrite and humble spirit, to revive the spirit of the
humble, and to revive the heart of the contrite ones.

—ISAIAH 57:15

WE ARE EXPECTING *wonderful things from the Lord for 1907. It is a jubilee year. May we all spend it at His feet, learning of Him.*

The closing up of the old year and beginning of the new found us on our knees at Azusa Mission. And as the new year was announced, such a wave of glory, divine love, and unity came over us. The meeting went on all the next day.

The Lord did great things in 1906. Pentecost first fell in Los Angeles on April 9. Since then the good tidings have spread in two hemispheres. Many are rejoicing in pardon, purity, and the power of the Holy Ghost. Wherever the work goes, souls are saved, and not only saved from hell, but through and through, and prepared to meet the Lord at His coming.

They are being filled with the holy oil, the baptism with the Holy Ghost, and wherever they go, it is being poured out.

From the little mustard-seed faith that was given to a little company of people waiting on God in a cottage prayer meeting, a great tree has grown, so that people from all parts of the country are coming like birds to lodge in the branches thereof (Matt. 13:31–32). The faith is still growing, and we are still just in the beginning, earnestly contending for the faith once delivered unto the saints.

Have you ever participated in revival? If so, describe your experience. If not, write a prayer asking God for revival:

~~⚬⚬~~

_____

_____

_____

_____

_____

_____

_____

_____

Ask Yourself . . .

❖ Are you hungry for revival?
❖ Will you pay the cost for revival in repentance, prayer, spiritual discipline, giving, worship, and praise?

Write a prayer of praise for the coming revival in you, your church, town, and nation.

_____

_____

_____

Day 29

Rivers of Living Water

*He that believeth on me, as the scripture hath said,
out of his belly shall flow rivers of living water.*

—JOHN 7:38

IN THE FOURTH *chapter of John, the words come, "Jesus answered
and said unto her, If thou knewest the gift of God, and who it is
that saith to thee, Give me to drink; thou wouldest have asked of
him, and he would have given thee living water" (John 4:10). Praise
God for the living waters today that flow freely, for they come from
God to every hungry and thirsty heart.*

*We are able to go in the mighty name of Jesus to the ends of the
earth and water dry places, deserts, and solitary places, until these
parched, sad, lonely hearts are made to rejoice in the God of their
salvation. We want the rivers today.*

Jesus teaches the woman at the well, and us, the
importance of living water. We cannot survive spiritually
without the Spirit's flow of living waters into our lives.
How is the spiritual river flowing within you? Put an *x* on
the line where you are in your walk with the Spirit now:

Being refreshed in the Spirit   Stale in the Spirit

Dry and thirsty   Filled with the Spirit

Free in the Spirit	Hindering the Spirit

| Overflowing with the Spirit | Stagnant in the Spirit |

True revival flows in the river of God. His living water flows through His people and refreshes anyone who is thirsty for God.

N JESUS CHRIST *we receive forgiveness of sins, sanctification of our spirit, soul, and body, and upon sanctification we may receive the gift of the Holy Ghost that Jesus promised to His disciples, the promise of the Father. All this we get through the atonement. Hallelujah!*

The prophet said that Jesus had borne our griefs and carried our sorrows. "He was wounded for our transgressions, he was bruised for our iniquities: the chastisement of our peace was upon him; and with his stripes we are healed" (Isa. 53:5). We have healing, health, salvation, joy, life — everything in Jesus. Glory to God!

The living water of God in revival brings healing. Read Revelation 22:1–2. Rewrite this passage in your own words:

_____

_____

_____

Day 29

Ask Yourself . . .

❖   How is the river of God flowing in your life?
In your church?

❖   In what ways have you been healed by His
living water?

*Write a prayer asking Jesus to overflow you with His living
waters:*

_____

_____

_____

Day 30

Receive Ye the Holy Ghost

But the Comforter, which is the Holy Ghost, whom the Father will send in my name, he shall teach you all things.

—JOHN 14:26

THE FIRST STEP *in seeking the baptism with the Holy Ghost is to have a clear knowledge of the new birth in our souls, which is the first work of grace and brings everlasting life to our souls* (Rom. 5:1). *Every one who repents and turns to the Lord Jesus with faith in Him, receives forgiveness of sins. Justification and regeneration are simultaneous. The pardoned sinner becomes a child of God in justification.*

The next step is to have a clear knowledge, by the Holy Spirit, of the second work of grace wrought in our hearts by the power of the blood and the Holy Ghost. "For by one offering he hath perfected for ever them that are sanctified. Whereof the Holy Ghost also is a witness to us" (Heb. 10:14–15). *We have Christ, crowned and enthroned in our hearts, the tree of life. We have the brooks and streams of salvation flowing in our souls, but praise God, we can have the rivers* (John 7:38–39). *Christ is now given and being poured out upon all flesh. All races, nations, and tongues are receiving the baptism with the Holy Ghost and fire, according to the prophet Joel* (2:28–32).

When we have a clear knowledge of justification and sanctification through the precious blood of Jesus Christ in our hearts, then we can be recipients of the baptism with the Holy Ghost.

Day 30

Describe how Jesus justified you: _____

_____

Describe how Jesus sanctified you: _____

_____

Describe the baptism of the Holy Spirit in your life:

_____

In reflecting over what you have learned in this devotional study, complete the following statements:

The reason I need reviving is _____

_____.

God desires to revive the church in order to _____

_____.

The Holy Spirit empowers me to _____

_____.

Five lost people that I love and will share the gospel with in the next month are _____

_____.

I need to repent of _____

_____.

I give God praise for _____

_____.

Ask Yourself . . .

- ❖ Are you ready to move beyond studying about revival to being revived?
- ❖ Will you pray persistently for revival?
- ❖ Will you surrender all every day to Jesus?

Write a prayer thanking Jesus for revival by His Holy Spirit:

_____

_____

_____

Leader's Guide

For Group Sessions

This devotional study is an excellent resource for group study including such settings as:

- ❖ Sunday school classes and other church classes.
- ❖ Prayer groups.
- ❖ Bible study groups.
- ❖ Ministries involving small groups, home groups, and accountability groups.
- ❖ Study groups for youth and adults.

Before the first session

- ❖ Contact everyone interested or already partic-ipating in the group about the meeting time, date, and place.
- ❖ Make certain that everyone has a copy of this devotional study guide, *The Original Azusa Street Devotional,* and the *Holy Spirit Encounter Bible.*
- ❖ Ask group members to begin their daily encoun-ters in this guide. Plan for six sessions with each group session covering five devotional studies. Group members who faithfully do a devotional each day will be prepared to share in the group sessions. Plan out all your sessions before starting the first session.
- ❖ Pray for the Holy Spirit to guide, teach, and help each participant.
- ❖ Be certain that the place where you will meet has a chalkboard, white board, or flip chart with

appropriate writing materials. It is also best to be in a setting with movable, not fixed, seating.

Planning the Group Sessions

1. You will have six sessions together as a group. Plan to cover at least five days in each session.
2. In your first session, allow group members to select a partner with whom they will share and pray during each session. Keep the same pairs throughout the group sessions. You can put pairs together randomly—men with men and women with women.
3. Begin each session with prayer.
4. Read or ask group members to read the key scriptures at the start of each daily devotional for the five days prior to that session.
5. Prior to each session, decide which exercises and questions you would like to cover from the five daily devotional studies for that session.
6. Decide which exercises and sessions will be most appropriate for your group to share as a whole and which would be more comfortable for group members to share in pairs.
7. From the five previous days, decide which prayer(s) you wish the pairs to pray with one another.
8. Close each session with each group member sharing with the total group how he or she grew in faith during the previous week. Then lead the group in prayer, or have group members pray aloud. Close the session with your own prayer.
9. In the last session, use the thirtieth day as an in-depth sharing time in pairs. Invite all the

group members to share the most important thing they learned about revival during this study, and how their relationship with the Lord was deepened during the study. Close with prayers of praise and thanksgiving.

10. Whether sharing in pairs or as a total group, remember to allow each person the freedom not to share if they are not comfortable.

11. Be careful. This is not a therapy group. Group members who seek to dominate group discussions with their own problems or questions should be ministered to by the group leader or pastor in a one-on-one setting outside of the group session.

12. Always start and end the group session on time, and seek to keep the session within a ninety-minute time frame.